HERITAGE CELEBRATIONS

A Guide to Celebrating the History of Your Church
Revised and Updated

by Wilma McKee

Faith & Life Press, Newton, Kansas

Library of Congress Number 93-73915

International Standard Book Number 0-87303-219-5

The Historical Committee of the General Conference Mennonite Church sponsored the research and writing of this book, which was first published as *Heritage Celebrations: A Resource Book for Congregations* (Faith & Life Press, 1992).

Editorial direction for Faith & Life Press by Susan E. Janzen; copyediting by Edna Krueger Dyck; design by John Hiebert; printing by Mennonite Press. Cover art by Joy Dunn Keenan.

CONTENTS

Preface

Why write a book on planning church anniversaries and other historical celebrations? We desired to encourage and stimulate congregations to reach out to God in praise and thanksgiving, to joyfully remember their Christian heritage, and to consequently gain a vision for their future mission. This book provides resources which will assist congregations in the various tasks involved in celebration.

Several concepts are significant:

1. The meaning of celebration needs to be broadened within congregations. Celebrations have often been limited to large anniversaries.

2. God's Word expresses clearly the necessity for celebration in all its various dimensions. The question needs to be asked, Why do congregations neglect to use their many opportunities to celebrate?

3. Congregations are diverse in size, organization, and gifts. Suggestions must always allow and encourage a broad range of choices in planning any celebration.

Numerous persons have contributed to this book. In November 1989 the Historical Committee of the General

Conference Mennonite Church met in Newton, Kansas, with five persons who had experience in planning church celebrations. In May 1990 another meeting in Akron, Pennsylvania, involved individuals who represented congregations affiliated with both the General Conference Mennonite Church (GCMC) and the Mennonite Church. We are grateful to all of these persons for their sound advice and encouragement.

Norma Johnson, executive secretary of the GCMC Commission on Education, met with the committee and gave supportive and wise assistance. Norma and Robert Kreider, chairman of the former GCMC Heritage Committee, read the manuscript on request.

During the writing process, Samuel Steiner, Ontario Mennonite Historical Society, Hope Lind and Levi Miller of the Historical Committee of the Mennonite Church, and James O. Lehman, Eastern Mennonite College/Seminary read one of the drafts of the book and made extremely worthwhile suggestions and comments.

Two books stimulated my thinking while writing: *Stories with Meaning, A Guide for the Writing of Congregational Histories* by Frank H. Epp and *Places of Worship, Exploring Their History* by James P. Wind (Nashville: American Association for State and Local History, 1990) from the Nearby History Series.

Members of the General Conference Historical Committee, David A. Haury, Topeka, Kansas, chairperson, Lawrence Klippenstein, Winnipeg, Manitoba, David Rempel Smucker, Akron, Pennsylvania, and Steven R. Estes, Hopedale, Illinois, assisted in formulating the book outline. Throughout the work on the resource book they critiqued the manuscript, assisted with decisions, and gave freely of their expertise. Most importantly they challenged and supported me. This resource book is only possible because of their valuable assistance.

I acknowledge the varied contributions of each of the persons mentioned above and offer my sincere thanks.

Wilma McKee

Chapter 1

WHY DO WE CELEBRATE?

Why do believers within the body of Jesus Christ feel the need to celebrate? Is it for entertainment and excitement? Is it to draw the attention of our neighboring congregations and conferences? Do we celebrate only out of selfish motivation, perhaps to make ourselves feel good?

God created human beings to celebrate. Christians celebrate every week when they come together on Sunday as well as other times they gather to worship. Their celebration is based on a relationship with Jesus Christ as Lord and Savior and on the creative acts of God in past, present, and future.

Called to Remember

We celebrate God acting in history in order to call to remembrance, to solemnize, to honor, to proclaim, and to praise. That which is celebrated becomes distinguished and extolled in our hearts and minds.

The Bible encourages us to celebrate. "This is the day

1

that the Lord has made; let us rejoice and be glad in it" (Psalm 118:24). In the Old Testament, God's people are to remember the early days. In Deuteronomy, they are told to remember how the Lord had led them, and to "remember the days of old, consider the years long past; ask your father and he will inform you; your elders and they will tell you" (Deuteronomy 32:7). In Isaiah 5l:1-2, the Israelites were instructed to "look to the rock from which you were cut. . . look to Abraham, your father, and to Sarah, who bore you."

The festivals of Israel were to be solemn, holy days with the purpose of commemorating the acts of God and keeping God central in the lives of the people. Occasions occurred when no one came to Israel's appointed feasts and the celebrations turned to days of mourning.

Strong warnings from the prophet Amos instructed the people that God hated their festivals when their hearts were not sincere. Justice and righteousness were to be the foundation stones of celebration. Always we see that solemnity of mind and purpose coupled with joy in the act of celebration.

In the New Testament, the woman who anointed Jesus in Bethany created a memorial to honor him (Matthew 26:6-13). Jesus spoke to his disciples of remembrance at the Lord's Supper, when he said, "Do this in remembrance of me" (1 Corinthians 11:24).

Christianity is fundamentally historical, based on the life, death, and resurrection of Jesus. Throughout history we have celebrated the living presence of Jesus in our congregations by commemorating the special events in his life, such as Christmas, Easter, and Pentecost.

Celebration includes not only remembrance, but appropriation of that which is remembered. We act on the basis of what has been taught us about the past.

We commemorate in order to create a memorial for those who come after us. Just as Joshua did when he placed the twelve stones in the Jordan River, so we must be able to tell all who ask what our stones of memorial mean (Joshua 4:6-7). To the believers of the past and today, celebration is a natural response to our Creator.

Praise and Thanksgiving

The word *celebration* is sometimes corrupted when used in a secular sense. However, to believers, it is richest as an expression of majestic praise.

The book of Psalms represents praise for many Christians with its emphasis on faith and trust. In the Hebrew language the psalms are called, "The Praises," even though many of them are prayers. They are used universally to glorify, magnify, and worship God. At their core is the unshakable belief that God is the center of life, of history, and of the whole creation.

In Psalm 42 the writer speaks of his thirst for the living God and remembers the days he led the multitudes in a procession to the house of God. He lifts out as memorable the shouts of joy and thanksgiving of the congregation.

Our congregations should not shy away from thanksgiving even though Thanksgiving Day, in the United States, has become secularized as a patriotic holiday. It is a part of our Christian heritage too. The spiritual health of the congregation requires that every event is a cause for thanksgiving. The lives of our members who have passed on, projects which have been completed, as well as answers to specific prayers are reasons to give thanks. One thing this book will do is broaden thanksgiving into a yearlong event which includes all of our past. Specific suggestions are given for doing this.

Clear Vision

We are given clarity of vision in celebration. We often seem unable to rise above the corruption and cynicism which surrounds us in our world and which prevents us from having a clear vision. It is dangerous to be without the protective influence of a clear and discriminating vision.

Our immediate needs work as blinders which keep us from seeing future blessings and possibilities for service. When our present needs are set aside in celebration, even briefly, our spirits are renewed and allow us to dream dreams and see visions (Joel 2:28) for our congregations.

The two-directional nature of history—we look both backward and forward—frees us for unusual discernment in the present. As we look to the past, we see revealed the magnitude of accomplishments, as well as the wisdom gained from failures, and the strength and patience developed from struggle.

We read that God gave many visions and told parables (Hosea 12:10) through people in their times of faithfulness. Paul was not disobedient to the heavenly vision (Acts 26:19), stressing again the action which follows faithfulness to godly insight.

As we look forward, we can be assured of God's revelation in our particular vision, and that it will come at the appropriate time. "If it seems to tarry, wait for it; it will surely come, it will not delay" (Habakkuk 2:3).

Forgiveness, Reconciliation, and Healing

As we approach the act of celebrating God at work in our past, we are often brought face-to-face with our need for forgiveness. This need for forgiveness may be between individuals, between an individual and the congregation, between segments of the congregation, or between one congregation and another. The reasons may have been long buried. Often people do not approach them openly and there may even be an unspoken agreement not to speak of them.

For example, when all former pastors are invited to participate in the celebration events, how do we handle the situation if one pastor left under a cloud of mistrust? How do we relate during the celebration to the family of former members where forgiveness was never achieved?

If a congregation decides to write its history and determines to present a true history of God working in its midst instead of simply an accumulation of facts, how does such a group deal with the "troubled areas"?

Some congregations prefer to "skip over" painful occurrences; others believe that reconciliation will be necessary before true celebration can happen. Another possibility is that reconciliation may occur within celebrations, such as in a communion service. Reconciliation changes relationships between persons when it causes movement from enmity to fellowship. All reconciliation arises out of changes induced by the action of God. On the other hand, an unrelieved sense of guilt is one of the major causes of illness in individuals and congregations.

Healing can follow as forgiveness becomes a liberating force and true freedom is experienced. It is best not to ignore divisions and conflicts and not to bury hurts. The psalmist David expresses the blessedness of forgiveness and the celebration which results: "Be glad in the Lord and rejoice, O righteous, and shout for joy, all you upright in heart" (Psalm 32: 11). Forgiveness turns us loose from yesterday to trust for tomorrow's mission.

Reaching Within and Without

Celebrations are an excellent way to reach out to others. We can contact those who have moved out from our midst for whatever reasons. We can look upon them as extended family. As they participate with us, they will recall their former commitments to God and within this congregation. Those fringe members can be drawn closer to us and experience a sense of belonging with us. New members will grow in commitment as they use their gifts within the congregation. We will want to include members who have come from different backgrounds in our celebration. We can encourage them to enrich us by sharing their heritage. In an exchange of culture and customs, and in joint worship, God will strengthen our bonds of love.

Other congregations of like faith will benefit from praising God with us. Other denominations will have a clearer understanding of us as fellow believers and will feel ties for the future as they share and celebrate with us. We can reach out to those who live in close proximity to us but who do not know our history or beliefs.

Celebration events can become times of true hospitality. Some persons in every community feel separated from God and the believers of all denominations for whatever reasons. They stand alone and are lonely. Friendships can be cultivated between families; griefs, joys and needs can be shared.

The Past Enriches the Future

When we ignore our past, we become vulnerable to repeating its mistakes. The light and darkness from the past provide a basis for sound judgment for the present and future. Without seeking to make them perfect, we can look at the lives of former members and learn from them. Those who began our congregations and those who nurtured us into being deserve our remembrance and thanks. In their labor we see the hand of God in our midst.

Jacob set up a stone (Genesis 28:18) to aid him in remembering his covenant with God. In like manner, heritage celebrations can use symbols to remind congregations of our former commitments.

How can any of us celebrate without the perspective of the past? History gives us a long-range view. As we become more aware of our own story, with all its joys and struggles, we may in the very act of celebration receive a fuller measure of grace to live as God's people.

The Congregation Working Together

The congregation doing the celebrating will perhaps reap the most benefits. In difficult situations, the celebration of God's praises in song or story can help us remain steadfast and secure in our faith. In times when all things are going well, celebration will recall to us our need to praise God and refocus our minds on what God is calling us to be and do in the world.

The benefits of working together in planning any celebration are an important added dimension. As we search out our past history, plan worship experiences and varied events, reach out both within and without our congregation, the resulting blessing is often togetherness and mutuality. We learn anew the value of patience, we see hidden gifts emerge, and we become aware in new ways of the meaning and value of fellowship and community.

Chapter 2

WHEN DO WE CELEBRATE?

Celebration in its broadest sense includes every act of worship. When we acknowledge that our chief aim is to give God glory and praise in all our actions, then reasons to celebrate in our congregations become limitless.

Celebrations may achieve various results. Some of the consequences are: the benefits of working together; the richness of corporate praise and worship; the factual sharing of the congregation's history; and the bonding of the congregation through celebration and witness to the community.

Each congregation needs to decide when to celebrate and what is appropriate within its group. A celebration should not become a once-in-a-lifetime experience. It is more than a repetition of what has been done. A celebration may be as simple as having an outside speaker and a service of praise or as extensive as an anniversary with planned, yearlong events. The same event will mean different things to different congregations and to various persons in the congregations.

Congregational Anniversaries

Celebrating an anniversary tends to establish and bond us together. Anniversaries cause us to look at where we have been and where we are going. With this in mind, a congregation may want to celebrate a one-year anniversary or any time span they choose. Do not wait for the twenty-fifth or greater anniversary. Added years will certainly enlarge the magnitude of what a congregation may celebrate. Events which seldom occur, such as a fiftieth or seventy-fifth anniversary, require extra planning and a longer preparation time. We commonly expect these anniversaries to be treated as important. (See Appendix A for a sample litany for a seventy-fifth anniversary.)

Building Anniversaries

The anniversary of a church building project can help the congregation remember times of working together and of sacrificial giving. This kind of celebration needs to be approached carefully to avoid reinforcing the idea that *church* and *building* are synonymous. Events of worship, study, and commitment have caused the building to evolve into more than a physical home for the congregation or as the sole location of God's presence.

The ground-breaking or cornerstone-laying ceremonies are occasions for commemoration. Invite representatives of the congregation and builders who took part in the original services to assist. Remember them with gratitude.

When a congregation lays a cornerstone, it will want to keep a list of the contents placed in it, for example: a history of the local church, list of present members, constitution, church bulletin, and yearbook. Original documents should be kept in safe conditions while copies can go into the cornerstone. (Anniversary programs may wish to use these documents as reminders.)

The first service in a new building is worthy of remembrance and celebration. What were the congregation's hopes and prayers for the usefulness of the building? In the same manner that Jacob built a pillar at Bethel and poured oil on it, so the congregation affirmed: This is God's house. Members originally dedicated these rooms for worship, for teaching, preaching the Word, for song, prayer, and for fellowship. At the time of remembrance, the congregation needs to be reminded of this commitment and to ask the question: Have these original hopes and prayers been fulfilled and answered?

We tend to celebrate beginnings of a present, ongoing reality, but we neglect the closure needed to free us for future involvement. Any closure needs to be celebrated in some way, whether the dissolution of a congregation, a minister's ending time of service, the demise of a mission project, or when long-term workers retire. Though often disregarded, celebrating these closure events can support the transition process.

Migration Anniversaries

Many congregations have come together because of migration from another country, state, province, or even a sister congregation. Stories can be gathered and shared of difficulties in travel, of struggles in the new land, or joys experienced in recognizing the need to worship together in a new place. Present migrations can be included, such as urban congregations which have joined together. Save these stories of God acting in our midst, so they can be retold for children, youth, and new members.

Special Group Anniversaries

Groups within the congregation, such as women's, men's, youth, or music groups, can celebrate their beginnings and their contributions. These events can be used to thank God for persons who have served in nurturing positions. Celebrating group anniversaries often stimulates future growth and provides natural opportunities to define primary goals and to evaluate present work. Programs prepared for the congregation will acquaint them with the group's work. Possible questions to ask are:

1. Does the group's program provide social, spiritual, and service opportunities for its members?
2. Is there an area of service being overlooked?
3. Is there openness to new members?
4. How shall we make people feel welcome?

Sunday schools have a recognized value in a congregation. Many groups had their early beginnings in Sunday school classes. Often they have been seen as teaching and nurturing agents. They took on added importance as the church-controlled schools closed in some areas. Daily Vacation Bible Schools sometimes grew directly out of the desire to teach the Bible to children. Sunday schools have much to commemorate: the beginning, the formation of a particular class, the change in language, or the programs which may be outgrowths of the Sunday school such as Children's Day and Christmas Eve programs.

Mission Project Anniversaries

Mission projects have played a vital role in shaping the

identity of many congregations. How can we encourage the celebration of these missions?

1. The project's beginning, its special accomplishments, or its closing can be remembered.
2. Who suggested the project? Who was involved? Who has been affected by the results?
3. Older members can tell stories which are tape-recorded or written in story form for the congregation's library.
4. Dramas, musical programs, or a readers theater piece will serve as aids to remembering and celebrating.

What are some of the mission projects in which our congregations have had a part?

1. sending and supporting missionaries, overseas and at home
2. planting an urban church
3. food bank
4. nursery schools
5. day-care centers
6. clothing, craft shops
7. prison ministry
8. nursing-home ministry
9. cross-cultural projects
10. children's clubs
11. youth recreation centers

The congregation, including children, youth, and new members, need to see how these mission projects bring fresh life and vitality to the congregation. The release of creativity, the benefits of continual working together, and most of all the realization that God has used us to reach out to others are causes for celebration!

Combined Projects

Several congregations may have worked together on a special project. Perhaps many of the projects listed above have been joint efforts. What has your congregation done in cooperation with others? Has it planted a new group, started a Sunday school, established a nursing home, cooperated in a Bible school, or helped in relief projects?

Have there been joint services in your home community? Have the youth of the community planned combined projects? Working together builds rapport between congregations, whether it is an evangelistic event, a relief project for the community, or united prayer for hurting and grieving families.

Have you considered celebrating the anniversary of your congregation joining an area conference or other adjudicatory of your denomination? This membership makes many joint projects possible which would have failed as individual ventures. Such cooperation encourages and enables congregations to broaden relationships and strengthens the conference, producing a more effective witness.

Other Celebrations

Every part of congregational life is worthy of celebration. Some important and major events require much planning. Other events will not necessitate the same amount of structuring but are important to celebrate nevertheless.

Have you given money for a special project? Have you sent a missionary or voluntary service worker? An engagement, a marriage, the birth of a child, a baptism, communion, or a time of service given by a person of any age can be thought of as times to celebrate. Consider a funeral or memorial service as a time for celebration with its grief and remembering, its joy in the love which has been given and received. Has some event affecting an entire town or region had a special impact on your congregation?

A celebration is a desire to praise and give God glory in all things. Celebrations teach us about past events, allow us to evaluate goals and renew commitments. When congregational life is celebrated, struggles and joys will be revealed, but we will more clearly see God at work.

Chapter 3

HOW DO WE PLAN A CELEBRATION?

S tart early. Congregations beginning to plan any kind of celebration should look realistically at options including the extent and duration of events. Will this be a one-hour, one-day, weeklong, or yearlong event? Some congregations neglect to begin early enough and as a consequence "short circuit" their results. Planning for an anniversary needs to start very early, with the timing determined by the complexity of the celebration. A time table which can be revised as the planning progresses will be a valuable tool.

It is not advisable to combine all of a celebration into one long event such as a Sunday morning service. Several shorter programs on one day or even extending the celebration over several days or months can be more effective. If planning starts early, the celebration will be more meaningful to the congregation, and momentum and enthusiasm will build.

Select a Steering Committee

Initially, most congregations will want to select a

steering committee. No one way exists for selecting this committee. Each congregation will follow its own pattern in making appointments. Its composition should depend on the responsibilities involved. All planning will be coordinated by this committee, although other committees and individuals will be deeply involved. In some congregations a historian and/or historical committee will be a natural part of the steering committee.

In many congregations the pastor will be a member of the steering committee, depending on gifts and time available. In the event that none of the ministers serves on the committee, the pastoral leadership needs to be fully informed and supportive of the endeavor.

Ask for Help

The steering committee may wish to ask for someone with experience in planning celebrations to meet with them and to discuss and list options. Possible consultants would be adjudicatory staff and historical committees or local historical society members. Such helpful consultation could occur at any time during the planning period or during the actual celebration events. With many and diverse options, more satisfying choices will be possible.

Involve Congregational Leadership

At an early date, the steering committee will be ready to meet with the congregation's governing body to listen and discuss the limitations and priorities of the celebration. Do the members of the governing body understand the reasons for the celebration? Chapter 1, "Why Do We Celebrate?" may be helpful in building understanding.

How long before the anniversary shall the celebration

events begin? Will several days, months, or even a year of occurrences be scheduled? Some options could include:

1. a weekend of events culminating on Sunday
2. a month or several months of events including sermons, bulletin inserts, and programs before the primary anniversary
3. a yearlong celebration including all groups within the congregation. The theme of the anniversary would be incorporated into the congregation's calendar. For more detailed suggestions for scheduling and events, see chapters 5 to 8 of this book.

What are the budget implications which may limit the anniversary expenses? Will the general budget be able to accommodate the extra cost? Should the anniversary celebration pay for itself or for part of the expense by selling books, tapes, or meals? A clear understanding at the beginning will avoid misunderstandings later in the celebration.

Inspire the Congregation

How will the congregation become enthusiastic about the project? One may invite an appropriate speaker to present the reasons and needs for celebration. Persons who were involved in the congregation's beginnings or other anniversary celebrations may be invited to speak on exciting events from the congregation's past. Storytelling is an inspiring addition to any celebration. It appeals to all ages and has a wide range of possibilities. Use short, well-written tidbits, biographical sketches, or brief stories from the past to whet the congregation's appetite.

Tailor the celebration to draw on a wide diversity of

gifts, including those not usually used. Do not give up on involving the congregation or on working for their enthusiasm. Even though a few persons may choose not to cooperate with plans, go ahead, realizing you will not always receive one-hundred percent cooperation. Mutuality may grow during the events. Help convince the unconvinced by explaining that the celebration assists in preparing the congregation to not only look to the past, but to the present, and toward the future.

Set Goals

With these initial understandings and emerging enthusiasm, the congregation can now help to develop goals for the celebration. When the congregation is involved in formulating early ideas, it will more likely "own" the celebration and therefore support and reap the diverse benefits of it.

Select a Theme

The steering committee may decide on the anniversary or celebration theme. This theme could give important direction to the entire celebration. It may become a focal point, helping the congregation to channel its efforts, including worship toward one central emphasis. The theme should be broad enough to cover all important aspects but still focused enough to give clarity of meaning.

Appoint Key Committees

The steering committee will appoint other key committees. Individual help may be sufficient in some areas and fewer committees may be necessary. Each committee or individual needs to understand clearly the responsibilities involved. Examples of committees many celebration events may need are:

1. program
2. food
3. publicity
4. decoration
5. music
6. drama
7. historical collections, including documents and photographs
8. exhibits
9. publications

Clear and continuing communication between the steering committee and other committees and individuals is crucial. This helps prevent duplication and potential conflict.

Promote the Celebration

Ideas to promote the entire celebration will need to be discussed early. How will the events be publicized?

1. Distribute news releases.
2. Prepare special bulletin inserts.
3. Write stories for denominational papers.
4. Write stories for local newspapers.
5. Reach nonresident and former members through an enthusiastic newsletter.

The celebration event will have every chance to be successful if the congregation begins planning early and has goals clearly formulated. The involvement of many persons with diverse gifts and an enthusiastic congregation will add exciting momentum. Promoting such an event seems a natural result.

Chapter 4

WHOM WILL THE CELEBRATION INVOLVE?

The members of the congregation who are involved with the celebration will probably receive the greatest benefits. Is there a danger of involving too many persons in planning one event? When committees are too large they may become cumbersome, and members with busy schedules may have difficulty finding a time for meetings. Several persons may eventually do the work of the whole committee. A committee of appropriate size needs its responsibilities clearly defined. Having several committees may work better than having one large one.

A danger also exists of too few persons being involved. This results in a small group "owning" the celebration without the congregation as a whole shouldering the responsibility or fully enjoying the celebration as their own.

Groups to Be Involved

An anniversary celebration may involve the entire

congregation, while a smaller event may target one specific age or organizational group. Any organization, such as a Sunday school class, Bible school, children's, youth, men's, or women's group may plan a celebration. For example, if an adult class has successfully carried out a project, then at some interval, perhaps a six-month or one-year anniversary, they will benefit from celebrating their efforts with the entire congregation.

Special music or drama groups may plan a time of thanksgiving or remembrance. Many organized groups do valuable work but do not consider celebrating their efforts or sharing them with the larger church family.

How long have the women in your congregation worked faithfully in caring and sharing projects? Have they celebrated together and with other members of your congregation? Have they planned a time of remembrance with other neighboring organizations, sister congregations, or the community?

Involve Former Members

Past members often experience joy when included in a congregation's special celebrations. They may feel a sense of aloneness away from the group which in childhood or at some phase of their lives was extremely meaningful to them. An informal time when former members reflect and share on past events can add depth to the celebration. For example, they can share answers to questions they have been given in advance:

1. Tell us about the work you are doing at present.
2. What news of your immediate family would you want to share with us?

3. What congregation do you worship with now and what are your involvements or responsibilities?
4. What do you value specifically from your present congregation?
5. Which experiences from your years with the celebrating congregation do you value?
6. What changes do you see in the congregation since your absence?
7. What wisdom would you like to share with the celebrating congregation?

One or two questions could be chosen for a focus, if time is limited.

Involve Former Ministers

Ministers from the past life of the congregation can participate in special events in various ways as they stir up remembrances and help in commemorative events. Before the actual day of celebration, they can give Sunday morning sermons. They can assist in serving communion or in worship services. If the former minister is no longer living, the spouse and family could be invited to participate.

Ministers have often served in several congregations in different areas and may have gained some clarity of vision due to these broad experiences. If the celebrating congregation is open to insights, members can ask questions of a former minister or a panel of ministers which may help them to increase in self-knowledge. Suggested questions:

1. What do you remember from your time with us as some strengths of our group?
2. Do you see areas that need enriching?

3. What changes do you see over the years?
4. What are favorite remembrances from your time as our minister?
5. What is your prayer for this congregation?

Involve District and Conference

The history of how and when the celebrating congregation became a member of the denomination can be written or told in stories. How did this happen? What were the reasons for desiring membership? What are the goals we share with the larger group? What does the denomination need from us? What do we need from them? How can we enrich one another for ministry.

Which leaders can we ask to assist in our celebrations? Perhaps the chairperson of the regional historical committee or other committees, outside speakers knowledgeable about our history, or a person involved with a present mission project could inspire our planning and/or celebration.

Involve Other Congregations of Same Denomination

We value words of encouragement from other congregations. Sister groups may be a part of our thanksgiving and praise as they support us with their presence, their prayers, or with special input from individuals and musical groups.

Are there additional benefits we can gain through their involvement? Using their insights, can we see more clearly how other congregations view us?

Involve Congregations of Other Denominations

Other denominations can be involved through the local ministerial alliance. Informed persons can tell of local projects and accomplishments. In chapter 2, we have talked about combined projects, some of which are with congregations of different denominations. Fellowship increases cooperation and enthusiasm will be strengthened as we work and celebrate together.

At times, in informal settings, members of other denominations welcome the opportunity to ask questions about our beliefs and customs. Often we know surprisingly little about other denominations even in the same community. Would an informal program before the main celebration lend itself to this type of sharing?

Involve Those Outside All Congregations

How can we involve persons who are not Christians or do not take part in any congregation? Personal invitations from friends gain results more than general announcements. If background, culture, or race happen to be different, this can be an asset and may be used as a major opportunity. In informal events we can invite others to share their stories and customs with us. In all efforts to involve various people in our celebrations, we must remind ourselves that inclusiveness is clearly a virtue.

Chapter 5

WHAT PRELIMINARY PLANNING WILL BE NEEDED?

Preliminary planning must start early. Congregations limit themselves by not beginning early enough. What is an adequate time span? This question can only be answered by determining the extent and duration of the celebration. Effective planning depends on these two prior decisions.

1. How extensive will the celebration be?
2. How long will it last?

A congregation's governing body must be involved at an early date to select a steering committee and to make primary decisions with the steering committee.

What is the congregational historian's role in the celebration? The historian should be able to make a worthy and necessary contribution and will possibly be a valuable member of the steering committee. Due to the nature of their work and gifts, they will have a vital interest in an anniversary or other celebration. The historian will have records available and be able to assist in research.

It is critical to have the encouragement of the pastoral leadership. The steering committee requires a person who has organizational and administrative ability. The congregation can help decide the priorities and ways to work within the limitations of the congregation.

Scheduling a Short Celebration

A steering committee is helpful for any celebration. For one- or two-day events the congregational leadership may serve in this capacity. By calling upon established committees for decisions on food, decorations, and music, needed work can be accomplished without extra organization. A special group planning a celebration to highlight their organization and its mission may serve as their own steering committee.

A historical time line is an extremely valuable tool. It should cover the congregation's initial organization up to the present and include all groups within the congregation, the dates and details of their beginnings, and important changes in their work throughout the years. The congregational historian, if one exists, is the logical person to prepare this tool. If the congregation has not designated a historian, a volunteer may prepare a time line. A time line will assist all leaders and groups to easily find facts and prepare programs for celebration. (A sample of a historical time line is included in Appendix B.)

Any group planning a celebration must carefully consider the congregation's yearly calendar when scheduling events in order to avoid confusion and overlap.

Scheduling an Extended Celebration

Separate historical and program committees will probably be needed in a larger celebration which contains a series of events. Both will coordinate assignments with the steering committee. The historical committee's involvement includes: assisting in research, making facts available to other committees, searching out beginning events, and documenting the important changes through the years.

The program committee will plan preparation events and special programs of all kinds, including main celebration events.

The minimum time for planning would be twelve to eighteen months before the main celebration event. If the congregation plans to write or have written a detailed history, the time needs to be extended. A substantial book will take from two to five years to gather information, to write, and to publish. The decisions about the type of history and other commissioned items such as a hymn or drama which need special time and gifts are discussed in chapters 7, 9, and 10.

Chapter 6

HOW DO WE PREPARE THE CONGREGATION?

The preparation period for the main celebration will do more than assign tasks to members. It will bind the congregation together and join present members to former generations by giving hope for the future.

The natural desire of all persons to participate in a caring group will aid the congregation in their aim of inclusiveness. Today some congregations have single-parent or blended families. The church family can provide a meaningful identity for them as they become a part of special programs and events. Feelings of loneliness will be alleviated by a sense of belonging and values will be shared. Rituals can be used in celebration events to give a sense of continuity with the past and the future.

Rituals are essential and comforting to us in a world which changes constantly. Care must be taken not to make rituals an end in themselves, nor to allow them to exclude instead of include. New members can be encouraged to suggest rituals which they feel will bind the group together.

The history committee can make lists of interesting stories and events from the past which will provide ministers and various groups with ideas for topics for sermons or programs. Perhaps the library could purchase books about denominational history or related subjects at this time.

Use the celebration theme often in regular and special events. It will reach those on the periphery of planning.

Time Line of Preparation Events

The steering committee will need to make a time line of preparation events for the congregation. Although difficult to do so long before the main celebration, it can be expanded later.The time line will arouse interest and enthusiasm; be a convenient planning tool for all involved; and center the congregation around a common purpose.

Time Line for Eighteen Months of Planning

Eighteen months—Appoint steering committee.

Seventeen months—Meet with congregational leadership. Make decisions on events which need long-term planning and require special gifts and time. (See chapter 7.)

Sixteen months—Prepare congregation for celebration; use stories and sermons.

Fifteen months—Set goals with congregation. Select theme.

Fourteen months—Appoint other key committees.

Twelve months—Begin events which prepare congregation.

(Note: The usefulness of this time line will depend on

the scope of events.)

Sunday Morning Worship

Sermons on heritage celebration by the minister will prepare the congregation for future events. Other ideas for preparation in the worship time include the following:

1. Invite former ministers.
2. A pulpit exchange may add a challenge for the group.
3. Musical groups could prepare hymns which they remember learning when they were children.
4. Members might read favorite Scriptures.
5. Additional worship aids such as calls to worship or congregational prayers will distinguish the Sunday morning service.
6. Stories from the congregation's past or larger church history may be used during children's time.
7. Place items of historical interest in the bulletin.
8. A unique, especially designed bulletin cover will carry out the theme of the celebration.

Sunday School

Adult Sunday school classes may choose to use a series of lessons on the history of the congregation or denomination. Classes may want to study particular men and women who stand out as examples of the faith. A congregation may choose to design their own Sunday school curriculum for a month or even a quarter.

Past Records

Planning celebration events will remind the congregation of the importance of preserving records. A concerted effort by everyone will often result in finding valuable record books or minutes which have been misplaced.

Trustees or members who were involved in church building may present a review of original plans and costs and use these to emphasize the meaning of the building and its unique features. What needs were experienced at the time of building? Were these fulfilled? Have they enabled the congregation's program to thrive?

As treasurers review early financial records, changes throughout the years will become obvious. All groups in the congregation may find that reports on early organizations stimulate their memories. Records of significant congregational decisions in the past can reveal the pattern used to arrive at resolution. Do we need to change our decision-making methods?

Records of former celebrations will bring to mind stories of anniversaries and days of commemoration which can be shared with new members, youth, and children.

Special Programs

Noteworthy programs during the months before the main celebration event will stimulate and prepare the congregation.

The local historical society can be invited to give a program. The settlement of a particular area, its problems and successes, are a part of the life of the congregation and have had an effect on it.

A festival of praise can grow from what has caused the congregation to lift their hearts unitedly in praise to God. Remembering births, baptisms, or marriages can inspire themes of praise. Past and present reasons for

thanksgiving are so numerous that ideas for praise festivals are limitless. Specific topics will provide a better
focus than using too many topics at the same time.

A weeklong series of programs is often a part of the
congregation's calendar. Consider planning these meetings
with the celebration event in mind.

1. Could a congregational or professional historian
   be used in a program?
2. Are evangelistic services aimed toward the congregation's future mission appropriate?
3. Would a series, using members to tell their own
   stories of the congregation at work, encourage the
   entire group?
4. Unique evening programs can be based on members giving their own religious pilgrimages, using
   art media, drama, or music. Symbols for birth,
   growth, training, or service can be used in telling
   one's story. These stories of faith tend to bind the
   congregation together.
5. Sunday evening programs held in a cemetery may
   provide a healthy way of drawing several generations together. Stories of former leaders in the congregation or of family members can be told and
   their favorite songs can be used. Stories of humorous happenings, hobbies, and contributions to
   congregation and community will help adults,
   youth, and children to share in group experiences.
   As children take part in these informal services,
   they lose some of their fear of death. They feel
   comforted in the loss of family members when
   they hear people share stories which clearly show

that those who are not with us physically are still an important part of the congregational family.

Events Planned by Special Groups

Men's, women's, youth, and children's groups can plan preparation events throughout the year as part of their regular program. Adults may choose from various options:

1. Write a biography of charter members.
2. Plan an old-fashioned program.
3. Write stories or litanies of their group's organization and life.

Youth may help the congregation to prepare in the following ways:

1. Interview and write or tape life stories of an older member.
2. Make posters to publicize special programs and events.
3. Design a logo for the celebration.
4. Write a script which presents ideas about early congregational life.

Involve children in every aspect of the celebration. In this way we teach them that the past is a part of them and of their future.

1. Adults give children an understanding of some of their cultural and religious identity through ceremonies.
2. Children can prepare a service for the congregation. With their leader's encouragement they can write prayers, read Scripture verses, and sing songs. They may each share with the congregation their thoughts of what is important in life.

3. Encourage children to use objects such as dolls dressed in old-time clothes or old farm machinery.
4. Let children draw symbols for the group.
5. Children can make simple gifts for former ministers, visitors, or older members.
6. Let children help serve a meal, or make and decorate special cookies.
7. Show children pictures of former members and ministers in order to acquaint them with fore-sisters and brothers in the faith.
8. Help children prepare a family tree of ministers who have served the congregation, using pictures.

Special Days

Any major religious holiday on the calendar can provide an occasion to emphasize the history of the congregation or the biographies of Christians from the past.

Holidays such as Christmas, Easter, and Pentecost lend themselves naturally to celebration since they are the historical basis of Christianity. As preparation events, they speak of birth, sacrifice, new life, and the guidance of the Holy Spirit in the congregation's ongoing life.

Repeat a program, perhaps a Christmas play or cantata, which was given in previous years.

Annual events such as Mother's Day, Father's Day, Children's Day, or a Festival of the Christian Home may be used to speak of mothers and fathers in the Bible and of those who parented the congregation in its infancy and now. Questions can be discussed:

1. What are the qualities which we look for in a nurturing parent?
2. How has God used these parents in our congregation?

3. What is the place of children in our congregation?
4. How has God spoken to us through children and youth?

Chapter 7

WHICH EVENTS NEED LONG-TERM PLANNING?

C hapter 6 suggested programs and projects for morning worship, Sunday school, and other events which could be used many times. However, at an early stage the steering committee will recognize that some projects need long-term planning to achieve success. These may be onetime events.

This chapter will speak to onetime projects requiring special time, planning, and gifts. They call for preparation before the main celebration event. The decision to include or to avoid such projects may depend largely on available gifts in the congregation.

1. Is there a person(s) gifted in this area?
2. Do these persons have the necessary time for the project?

Special Gifts of Congregational Members

Make a list of members' gifts available for these events. Such a list can be expanded at any time to include

neglected gifts which are not commonly used or appreciated. Remembering people's hobbies can draw forth a gift
or talent.

1. Are there writers in your congregation? In chapter 10 we deal with writing a congregational history, but similar gifts of organization of thought
   and expression in the written word will be needed in several projects which call for summaries,
   scripts, or litanies. Perhaps a number of persons
   have these gifts.
2. What are the musical talents of the members,
   both young and old?
3. Are there members with artistic skills?
4. Designate a person to work with the sound system.
5. Select a carpenter to make scenery or models.
6. Is a member especially experienced in photography?
7. Who is gifted in working with publicity?
8. Can someone direct dramas?
9. Which leader can involve the youth and children?
10. Who has a gift for outreach and including others?

When persons are encouraged to use their gifts, both the
individual and the congregation receive an added blessing. The joy which comes from involvement is essential to
celebration.

Recording All Events

Events during the preparation months, as well as the
main celebration, should be recorded in some way. A person who is responsible for this should be appointed at an
early date. This person can ask others more competent in

using some kinds of media for help. Some forms for "recording" events are still photography, scrapbooks, cassette tapes, and videos.

Recorded materials can be used as part of the celebration. Then, when placed in the church library they can be used in follow-up programs years later. They will add valuable information to the congregation's historical records. Denominational archives may also want some of these materials.

Commissioning a Hymn

Would a hymn, composed especially for a celebration event, enhance the experience for your congregation? Will it add value in the years ahead as it serves to remind people of this particular worship service? Will it be a means of thanksgiving and praise to God?

As mentioned earlier in this chapter, do you have a person or persons who are gifted in music? Sometimes one person may be able to compose the lyrics and another the melody. A choir might sing the hymn for the main celebration event. A hymn for children or youth or perhaps a congregational response could be composed.

The planning committee may commission someone outside the congregation to undertake this project.

Performances Featured During the Celebration

The writing of a drama or other work could be among the early assignments. The following are some suggested topics:

1. the history of a denomination or the beginning and development of the local congregation
2. a pageant using story, script, and music about any

period of time in the congregation's history, or one showing progression of the congregation's history from past to present

3. a play about the beginning of the congregation for children to perform

4. skits of events:
    *   a church feud and how it was settled
    *   the discussion—both pros and cons—on a new program or project
    *   early settlers as they experienced difficulties from drought and crop failure
    *   experiences of neighboring families or of families helping one another in times of crisis

Youth often enjoy taking historical events and performing skits about them. They do this with good humor and creativity which older members accept and appreciate. History is learned, plus talents are discovered and developed in the process.

Organizing Displays

Displays may cover a wide range of topics. They can be composed of objects owned by the congregation which need to be collected and arranged or they may be newly constructed. The following are some suggestions:

1. pictures of families in the present congregation
2. pictures of charter members
3. pictures of ministers past and present
4. pictures drawn by children on what the celebration means to them
5. book displays: early record books, songbooks, old readers or other textbooks, materials used in Bible schools, earliest books from the library or Sunday

school literature

6. antiques: furniture used in homes; early church furniture, such as a pulpit, communion table, pews, or communion cups

7. artifacts: homemade products such as items which were used in early services.

8. banners: these add to the uniqueness of a service and can deal with a theme such as celebration, joy, praise, or thanksgiving. They can also list names of charter members or communities from which charter members first came. They can represent the congregation at work and worship by making banners of the holidays in the church year.

9. quilts: older ones can be used or if a quilt has been made for various ministerial families through the years, these can be borrowed and displayed. A quilt can be made especially for the celebration depicting events in the congregation's history. This quilt could then be left on display after the celebration events.

Publishing a Cookbook

A committee may decide that now is an opportune time to collect recipes from members for a cookbook. Items of history or a brief summary about the family contributing the recipe can be added. Establishing guidelines, gathering recipes, typing, editing, organizing, and choosing a publisher are all parts of the work which goes into making a cookbook. Again, with this project you need to start early.

Souvenirs of the Celebration

Visitors as well as members of the congregation may enjoy a memento of the special occasion. Commemorative plates or mugs can be designed and ordered for the main event. Other souvenirs might be pictures of the past or present church buildings; shirts with special designs; or a folder containing a typed summary of celebration events through the preceding months with a descriptive paragraph of each. If a history is not being written, a folder on the main events of the history and a listing of present and past members could be prepared.

Youth Contests

The youth of the congregation may wish to have a creative writing contest. Interest can be stimulated by printing a list of possible topics and afterward having a celebration party to reward their efforts. These stories can be read to the congregation or printed in booklet form for the church library.

If the congregational history is being written, the youth, and others, could have a contest to select the title of the book.

Preparing Onetime Program Events

Prepare slides and commentary. Slides can be made of family groups, present or past, with suitable written commentary. Slides of Sunday school classes, women, men, youth, children, or music groups can be prepared with script.

If the congregation has members talented in making slides, direct them to events from history or the church calendar, such as a slide program on various Christmas

Eve or Children's Day programs which your congregation has celebrated. Persons in the congregation will often have taken snapshots of these events from which slides can be made.

Plan retreat programs for various age groups. Children and youth can have longer retreats during the summer, using as their theme stories about heroes from the history of their faith. Use drama to portray important events and coordinate with outings on the theme.

For newer members have a program on congregational development, not just the beginnings.

Constructing Models

Has the congregation worshiped in several different buildings over the years? Models of these buildings can be an effective display. Other types of models of early furniture, machinery, buggies, and other means of transportation can be added. Models of early types of heating stoves or lamps would be effective.

Planning Tours

Be sure to prepare a printed itinerary for self-guided tours. Include first worship site, first church building site, homes of early leaders, homes of charter members, cemetery, and other places of importance to the congregation. Include in your itinerary historical and interesting facts about each tour stop.

Communicating the Celebration

Letters to former ministers and members should be sent out at least six months in advance. Follow-up letters will remind them of main events and also tell of preparation events.

Making Important Decisions

From time to time the planning committee will need to make difficult and perhaps controversial decisions. They can never all be anticipated.

Some groups decide to pay travel expenses of former ministers for speaking at preparation events or for those who can attend the main celebration event. Other groups do not pay expenses.

Any congregation should carefully choose the projects and events they intend to use based on their time, talent, and finances. Time does limit choices, but when gifted persons become involved, they will often find the time. Their efforts will certainly add to making the celebration events an appreciated and long remembered part of the congregation's story.

Chapter 8

WHICH EVENTS NEED SHORT-TERM PLANNING?

Timing is important in any celebration. If the celebration stretches over too long a time period, will the main events be anticlimactic? Be careful to prepare and stimulate the congregation but do not bring them to a saturation point too early.

Another pertinent warning is not to overcrowd the main celebration days. This is a temptation because some visitors will be able to come only on Sunday. If you pack any service too full, it becomes lengthy and the audience will lose attention and interest.

Some of the long-term planning in chapter 7 went into important projects and a time should be planned for their presentation during the main event.

How Much Time Is Needed?

Is a weekend adequate? Will Friday evening, Saturday afternoon and evening, and Sunday morning and afternoon be the available time slots? This may be too much for some congregations, while others will want to plan events for the entire week before the main Sunday celebration. The amount of time desired will naturally limit or expand your planning.

Publicity Is Important

Publicity has already been mentioned in chapter 7. This aspect cannot be overemphasized. Most persons and congregations need to be reminded before they have events firmly fixed in their minds and schedules. Effective publicity will include the following:

1. information about preparation events
2. information about main celebration events
3. information about communion services, history book, hymn, dramas, and other special projects
4. invitations for overnight guests
5. information about meals
6. events which include children, youth, and other ages in significant ways

Include on your list of people to invite:

1. charter members still living and their families
2. former members
3. former ministers and families
4. fringe members
5. persons who have shown a special interest in the congregation
6. local community
7. ministerial alliance
8. congregations of different denominations
9. congregations of same denomination who are neighbors

10. regional and denominational representatives

Record Main Celebration Events

Many people will take photographs; however, it is best to make one person officially responsible so that the congregation has an orderly photographic record.

The local newspaper will probably want to record the main events, both in picture and story. Contact them a few weeks before the events.

Denominational publications may not always be able to send a photographer and reporter. Designate a congregational member to write and send a story and picture to them.

An important part of recording is a guest book. It will provide a record of those attending each event and their addresses.

Plan Carefully

When planning short-term events of possibly two or three days, do not neglect to include events of interest for all ages:

1. Have "remembering" events for older members and guests.
2. For the middle-aged group have a smorgasbord of past, present, and future events.
3. Youth and children will like "action" events. They enjoy seeing their work displayed and hearing it mentioned.

Events will need to cover a wide range of topics and types of worship:

1. remembering key events of the past
2. thanksgiving and praise

3. reconciliation times
4. vision for the future
5. meditative, worship times
6. active worship
7. special commissioned projects

Friday Evening Suggestions

1. Have an old-fashioned service patterned after the order and content of early services.
2. Have a program at the first meeting place of the congregation— perhaps a schoolhouse or home. If the building is gone, meet at the site and tell stories of early settlers, charter members, or happenings.
3. Present a play prepared by youth or children.
4. Sing older hymns as suggested by congregation. Perhaps you can obtain old songbooks used in earlier years.

Saturday Afternoon and Evening Suggestions

1. Have a time for informal visiting and sharing.
2. Do a slide presentation. (See chapter 7.)
3. Prepare a traditional meal of ethnic foods.
4. If self-guided tours or a guided tour have been planned, Saturday afternoon might be an appropriate time.
5. Have an open house of the church building. Guide persons through the displays.
6. If a cookbook has been published, introduce it and credit those involved.
7. If a quilt with historical content has been made, demonstrate and explain the symbols.
8. Buggy or wagon rides will interest youth and children.

9. For Saturday evening, perform some of the specially planned events, such as a drama, pageant, or skits.

No set way exists to organize Friday or Saturday as long as you consider all ages and meet physical, social, emotional, and spiritual needs.

Sunday—the Big Day!

Plan carefully and prayerfully. Be aware that some visitors will come for only one day. Make this a day of praise and thanksgiving which will be remembered with joy. Again remember to include all ages. Some parts of the morning worship are important to include:

1. call to worship
2. litany of praise
3. choir music—the newly-commissioned hymn or some other hymns having special meaning for the congregation
4. names of charter members (in the litany)
5. sermon, meditation or time of sharing, or testimony
6. greetings from denomination, sister churches, local churches, or former members
7. communion service
8. prayers written by members of the congregation (of various ages) or visitors

Decorations will add to the festive mood of the day. Displays of banners or flowers can be used. Children could carry flowers as part of the opening and present them to older or charter members.

An elaborate Sunday meal may demand too much effort for the congregation. A limit exists as to how much members can do and still enjoy this important time. If the members are planning a meal for Saturday, hosting overnight guests, and also helping in program events, they may become overburdened. Perhaps the Sunday meal could be catered. Potlucks can work with enough time. Don't begin the afternoon service too early. Make these decisions in the light of what will promote the goals of the celebration.

On Sunday afternoon the committee may choose one important event as a closing. If a history of the congregation has been written, present the book then. Read selected parts of it to the audience. If several writers were involved, the audience would enjoy a panel discussion by writers on main topics or on gathering the material. Books could be distributed at this time. Also, the history could be presented in parts at each service during the weekend. Other souvenirs which have been prepared can be given to members and visitors at this time.

A Fitting Closure

How shall we bring the celebration to a meaningful climax?

1. Would the congregation like to share in an evening lunch together as many families have in the past after a time of visiting?
2. Is there another custom in the life of the congregation that has become a rich tradition?
3. Is the congregation ready to make an appropriate statement about moving into future missions?
4. A closing could use an older member to represent the past history of the congregation; an adult of

any age for the present; and a child as a symbol of the future. This would be a way to bring together all the stages of congregational life.

5. Some congregations may wish to use the communion service for a closing.

6. Congregation and guests may wish to move outside and stand in a circle (or around the sanctuary) while they sing a hymn which has been a favorite over the years, followed by a group benediction.

Let the closing experience be one of thanksgiving and praise; let it blend together forgiveness and healing; and let it reach out for future mission as it climaxes in joy and celebration.

Chapter 9

HOW SHALL WE PRESERVE THE STORY?

We shoulder the responsibility of preserving the story of how God has worked in our congregations. If we value our faith and wish to sustain it for future generations, then we must prove we are serious by recording our history.

Record keeping is an often neglected part of congregational work. Many persons in the congregation focus mainly on the present with their interest pointed to the future. They may consider the past only as the two previous generations, thus losing significant memory. Such persons do not give record keeping the attention it deserves.

Often an approaching anniversary makes the congregation realize the need for past records. Where are they? Have they been scattered carelessly? Has a long-term secretary or treasurer assumed the record books were his/her own, even when the job has been turned over to someone else? Members should have an "absolute" understanding that records of congregational life and organization belong to the congregation as a whole, not to any one member of the congregation. An organization needs to emphasize the fact that a work is not finished until records are put in order, updated, and passed on to the person taking over the responsibility. Sometimes an old record book becomes completed in midterm and a new one started. The old one may get carelessly placed in a closet or attic.

Safety Precautions Are Necessary

Are there safe places in the church building to keep records? Has the congregation discussed a central place and methods of collecting and preserving records? Does the regional conference or denomination have an archive which solicits congregational records?

Important records may need to be duplicated and one copy placed in fireproof storage. One may also obtain acid-free folders and envelopes which will prevent deterioration of valuable records. A well-planned filing system is necessary. Denominational archives may help congregations store records safely in an organized way and answer any questions.

Many records of early congregations have been lost when the church body dissolved. No clear understanding existed of how and where the records should be preserved. When this happens, valuable testimony of the congregation's witness is lost to future generations.

Oral History

Oral history contains information about traditions, customs, and reasons for the changes in congregational life. These may never be found in written minutes or formal documentation. Recording oral sources has both advantages and disadvantages.

The following are some advantages:

1. There is tremendous human interest material which comes to the forefront in oral interviews. It may not have been recorded on paper and could be lost forever.
2. Collecting oral history from individuals or a group is affirming to those being interviewed.
3. Old memories that come to mind often bring new opportunity to evaluate from the vantage point of the present.

The following are some disadvantages:

1. Memories are fallible.
2. Memories may be biased or selective.
3. People may be reluctant to share their memories.

Regardless of these dangers, oral memories need to be preserved. Sometimes secretaries or those in charge of minutes will purposely leave out different viewpoints in order to avoid controversy. Oral memories can help "fill in" what actually happened. Most of all they involve older members of the congregation and place a value on their unique memories.

Persons doing the interviewing will probably want to use a questionnaire as a tool. A copy can be given before the interview to the person or persons being interviewed. Family members can sometimes help an older person recall facts and dates, by asking questions of him or her. The "helper" should not suggest the "proper" memories.

The older person should not try to say what the interviewer wants to hear.

A tape recorder is a convenient tool for recording the interview. Some persons are inhibited by this and care must be taken to conduct the sessions in an informal manner. Often when memories begin flowing easily, the recorder is completely forgotten. If there is doubt about the accuracy of some information, other sources should be checked to substantiate the facts. Sometimes a panel of older members can be brought together for an interview. They often stimulate and bring to the surface one another's memories. (Sample questions for oral interviews can be found in Appendix C.)

Congregational Scrapbook

Scrapbooks of clippings related to church life will also help preserve the story. These may be from bulletins, local newspapers, or conference papers. Included may be anniversary programs and other times special to the congregation. In the same way parents preserve the factual details of a child's life, the congregation's birth, growth, and development can be recorded in a scrapbook. Care needs to be taken with commercial scrapbooks which are often destructive chemically to their contents.

Photograph/Picture Albums

A picture collection adds vital interest to the history of any congregation. What kind of pictures will be of value?

1. buildings in which the congregation has worshiped
2. ground breaking for new buildings

3. charter members
4. ministers and their families
5. projects of the group
6. family groups
7. baptismal classes
8. anniversary celebrations
9. Sunday school classes
10. various other groups within the congregation
11. special program events, perhaps from Christmas or Easter
12. outings such as congregational retreats or picnics

The children of the congregation will enjoy and learn from picture collections long before they are able to read a written history.

Perhaps the children have prepared slide programs of stories from the Bible. These can be filed and used again. Since the characters are from the congregation, they gain historical value along with being educational.

Many congregations make videos of noteworthy events. Often they are kept by individuals and may be lost to the church's records. Slides, videos, photo albums, and scrapbooks can all be filed in a central place to insure safety and availability.

Memoirs, Diaries, and Journals

Some members of congregations have memoirs written by their ancestors which describe migration to a different country and the struggles involved in early years in a new land. While these treasured accounts remain the property of family members, they also add valuable information to the congregation's records. Sometimes copies can be made with permission.

Each generation has those who keep diaries and journals. The congregation may want to encourage this ongoing record. Often these are personal. Are they appropriate for congregational records? We tend to feel uneasy about this idea. But when we think of several generations preceding us, we can see from a different perspective how much personal journals can add to our history. Today's memoirs do not seem important, but time passes quickly. One or two generations from now, how valuable will today's factual records be as they reflect on daily struggles and personal calls to faithfulness?

Gathering and Preserving the Story

Gathering and preserving congregational records is often neglected. Select a historian or a committee responsible for congregational records. These persons should have a "sense of history." They should have an aptitude for the work and be able to organize material. Above all, they must understand their responsibilities. Can such a chosen person do an annual check on records of all groups within the congregation?

Numerous records need to be preserved and updated. This is only a partial list:

1. official documents such as deeds and legal papers, cemetery plot records
2. minutes of all groups
3. membership lists—how received, date of removal and reason for loss
4. attendance records
5. annual reports—financial statements
6. births, deaths, marriages, baptisms, and ordinations
7. ministers' reports to congregation
8. reports of new projects

9. completed projects
10. ongoing projects such as Bible school
11. record books which may have been completed
12. correspondence that refers to congregational activities

Your congregation may prepare a history compilation page to be filed annually. One may record the major events of the year on a single page. (A sample is in Appendix D.)

Exhibits

An exhibit which can be placed in a convenient spot in the church building can help to inform all who view it of the congregation's story.

These may include the following items:
1. artifacts from the past, or seals which have been designed by a group
2. banners, quilts, or church models for an ongoing display
3. documents of the congregation's early history such as a copy of the first constitution, organizational records, or a cemetery plot diagram (These can be framed for an attractive exhibit.)
4. framed pictures of charter members or of early ministers

Reaching back into the past will help remind and instruct the present generation.

The preservation of congregational history takes on added importance to us when we realize that knowing and understanding the present depends on being able to reach back and connect with the past.

Chapter 10

SHALL WE WRITE A CONGREGATIONAL HISTORY?

M any congregations experience specific problems in this task. We need caution here, but not to the point where the decision to write or not to write is determined by fear. Wise planning, adequate time, and help from consultants can help avoid later serious difficulties.

Planning

Does the congregation have experienced persons who may contribute to writing a history? Face the question squarely and if the answer is no, ask for help. Your regional or denominational historical committees can make referrals.

Look at other congregational histories. Denominational libraries and many public libraries have samples. Take the time to look at options before you make important decisions.

If you decide to write a history, remember the entire project is intended:

1. to build unity within the present congregation
2. to recognize and value diversity within the group

3. to understand the purposes for which the congregation was started
4. to contribute to the congregation's self-understanding and vision
5. most importantly, to preserve the story

Usually a history will be written at a time when a special occasion such as an anniversary takes place. However, interest can evolve at any time, if motivated by a person or persons who have insight into the congregation's history, an appreciation for the value of keeping the story intact, and a gift for writing history. This can provide the spark needed to get the project underway.

Basic Questions

What are the models available? Will the book follow a chronological approach, using time periods to identify the movement? Frank H. Epp, in *Stories with Meaning*, suggests external (immigration, settlement, war) or internal (leadership, building, or program periods) reference points or a combination of both. Could a chronological approach be used as a starting place and then other questions be asked as the writer looks at changes which occurred or shifts in the life of the congregation?

Will the history be formulated around the organizations of the church and result in a chapter on the Sunday school, the choir, and each organization of the congregation? If the history covers a short period of time, would a *topical* approach be more appropriate?

What will be the nature of the history? Is it being written to tell only the pleasant happenings of the congregation? Must completeness be sacrificed? If so, can it appropriately be called a history? That is, is it only our story or is it God's story working through us?

Will the book preach a sermon aimed at converting its readers or is it the story of an imperfect people listening (and sometimes not listening) to God? Will the book primarily chronicle dates and happenings or will it look carefully at changes and development in the life of the congregation? Will it seek to discover and interpret the distinctive vision of the congregation? Will the book point out the congregation's place in the history of the local community?

Will the form chosen have the potential to express the particular character and "flavor" of the congregation?

Many questions should be asked.

How much time will be required to research all materials, to organize a book outline, and to write, edit, and publish the book? Can a time line be prepared? A time line of eighteen to thirty-six months, depending on how much time people are willing to devote to it and the extent of the project is suggested. (A sample time line for about eighteen months is in the Appendix E.)

What are the budget implications of the book? Is the congregation prepared to cover the expenses of travel for research, photocopying, or secretarial assistance? Should the writer or writers be given an honorarium, paid a salary, or volunteer the work with expenses paid? How about publishing costs? Will the book be sold to pay for all expenses?

If a book does not seem advisable, would a shorter historical pamphlet make sense? Besides a factual record, the uniqueness of the congregation could be stressed. Similarities and sharing with other congregations could also be a part of the historical pamphlet.

Research

Who will do the research? The church historian will be able to facilitate some of the research. Much of the material which needs to be gathered, as is listed in chapter 9, under "Gathering and Preserving the Story," should be easily accessible to the historian. A preliminary survey may uncover available sources.

A historical committee can provide valuable research assistance by gathering materials on specific topics.

What are the limits to the research? Begin gathering the records of the congregation itself. These records should be explored thoroughly. They will often contribute not only factual material but data for analysis of the congregation's development.

Cemetery records contribute helpful information. Private diaries, journals of former leaders, and reports to the congregation from ministers are other sources close to the members.

Resources do not need to be limited to congregational records. Minutes of regional or denominational meetings may shed light on decisions made. Libraries have collections of periodicals which may contain relevant articles. Local newspapers may have written stories on anniversaries and special events in the congregation's life.

The county courthouse will have records that may answer some questions—for example, land records or marriage records of early settlers. County or state museums sometimes have articles, pictures, or artifacts which lend interest and information. Are there visual materials such as charts, maps, and photographs, which members have and which can add completeness to the history?

Research will include the oral interviews which have

been recorded from older members of the congregation. Interviews can also be assigned on specific topics.

The historical committee can set guidelines and direct all research in a manner which broadens the scope and also provides principles to follow. All sources should be explored carefully.

Don't postpone interviewing older members, since time often runs out due to failing eyesight, hearing, memories, and death itself.

Are there lost records and documents? Quite possibly gaps exist in the congregation's records. Some research committees begin in church buildings and explore all possible storage areas. Because various persons have been responsible (or, unfortunately, no one), it is extremely easy to misplace important documents. Many congregations have existed for years without a designated historian.

When the possibilities of locating records in the church building have been exhausted, ask members and ministers to search their own attics and closets. Garage sales, auctions, or rummage sales may reveal Sunday school materials, postcards, and relics from early times as well as written histories or journals.

Often amazing objects will appear, but even if the lost records are not found, those who searched will be impressed by the importance for careful record keeping in the future.

Will some translating be needed? For congregations formed by immigrant peoples, records and other documents may be written in a language that is no longer spoken by most people in the congregation. This is as true for older established congregations as it is for recently founded congregations. If persons within the congregation cannot do translation, ask at the denominational archive for names of persons. Above all, do not put this off! Not only are the records needed now, but the usability of all records will be increased by having them in a language everyone can read.

How extensively will the book be documented? Documentation adds to the time and work involved in writing a book, but it also greatly increases its value and is necessary if published sources are quoted. Identifying sources extends the usefulness of the writing for all who read it. For those who wish to do further research, end-notes, footnotes, and bibliography are a necessity.

During the research, careful notes must be made. Photocopied, typed, or handwritten notes can all be used. Usually it is wise to record one piece of information on each paper using cards or half sheets. Accuracy is important as to the source, author, title, place of publication, publisher, date, volume, pages, and location. It saves time and effort to record this information at the beginning of the research rather than having to look it up later. There should be a separate bibliographical note on each source.

When doing oral interviews, record the name, address, date, and place of interview. Data notes can be organized by topic or chronologically.

The methods used to document are not as important as the accuracy. If you are not absolutely certain of the facts, they should be recorded as a "probability." From the research notes will come an outline for writing the book. Themes and subthemes will all develop out of the research.

Will a pictorial directory be included? Pictures make the book vital by filling it with life. While a picture album is certainly not a substitute for a history, incorporating pictures adds to the visual interest of any book. The historical committee could provide a guide for the selection of pictures.

Will biographies of charter members be included? In one sense, the lives of charter members are like stones in the foundation of the congregation. The beginning organization and subsequent development was dependent on them. Their life stories are a part of the larger story. Their achievements, failures, and beliefs, acted out in daily experiences, brought the congregation into being.

Family members can be given guidelines to use in writing life summaries of charter members. The author(s) can also interview descendants of charter members.

Do not be tempted to hurry research because you long to write the history. Ample time needs to go into research in order for the finished product to have depth and meaning. Research data reveals the uniqueness of the congregation. Take care to avoid merely accumulating facts. Research should reveal the congregation's personality and allow the reader to share intimately in the congregation's life, both past and present.

Writing

Who will write the history? Does the congregation include persons gifted as writers who have the time and desire to do the work? If there are not such persons, then a writer may need to be chosen from outside the congregation. One option might be to find a college history student or graduate student who will write the history as a class project.

Will the history be written by one person or a committee? Regardless of the choice, it needs to be emphasized that one person must assume responsibility for conceptualizing the outline, for interpreting the facts, and finally editing the story into final written form. If one person does this as the author, an advisory committee may assist her or him. If the history is written by a committee, one editor will still be needed to make the final decisions. The editor has to carry responsibility, though he or she may rely heavily on other writers or the advisory committee.

If a committee writes the history, avoid hazards by careful planning before the writing begins.

1. Articulate goals for writing the history.
2. Guidelines need to be firmly stated.
3. Each writer must have a clear understanding of his or her assignment.
4. Deadlines must be regarded as fixed and absolute. The writers must recognize at the beginning that they are making a commitment. If they do not have the time or energy available, then someone else should take the assignment.
5. The editor has final authority and responsibility.

The history book committee may have been assigned to work on research and will be of tremendous help throughout the writing process. They may be able to contribute to a careful outline and to decisions about the book following a chronological, topical, or combination outline. They will know time periods in the life of the congregation which make natural points of division.

Congregational workshops will help to involve many

persons and enrich the history. In workshops, members can look at the congregation closely for present character-istics. They can discuss the development from earliest beginnings and become aware of influences both external and internal which may have shaped the life of the group. Such workshops can greatly assist the writer. The writer or writers will ask some of the following questions:

1. In what location did the congregation settle?
2. Who were the charter members and what was their background?
3. Who were the early leaders?
4. In what type of buildings did they worship?
5. What were the problem areas?
6. Has the congregation been actively involved in larger denominational programs and outreach?

Facts are just the beginning of the story and many continuing questions need to be asked such as:

1. How did the location of the church shape the life of the congregation?
2. What were the theological emphases in the initial period?
3. What is the congregation's relationship to the sur-rounding churches? Is it usually in a leadership role or does it remain in the background or even aloof from other churches? What is the congrega-tion's role in local community history? Have members started new businesses or held responsi-ble positions in the community?
4. What were the turning points in the life of the congregation?

5. Were there times of crises which changed the congregation?
6. Were there slow, gradual changes?
7. Did outside events cause a shift in congregational
   life?
8. What has the congregation's attitude been toward
   missions outside the church? Is the group interested in social issues? Are they strongly evangelistic and what does this mean for the life of the
   congregation?
9. What are the rituals the congregation holds dear?

One should not judge a history on the basis of total completeness. Everything does not need to be included. Instead the writer should stand back and look at the over-all picture. What are the recurring patterns which reveal the identity of the congregation? In searching for these clues, the writer may feel like a reporter or even a detective. (Sample questions are in Appendix F.)

After reading the history will the reader feel in some way a part of the story? Does the particular vision of the congregation speak clearly? Do their successes, failures, and contributions reveal their particular identity? Can the reader discern God at work in the life of the congregation? Do some personalities and relationships speak so distinctly that they give reality to the story?

Editing

Who will edit the history? This is a large and important task which may require additional help.

1. A historical or advisory committee can help to
   check sources for accuracy.

2. A writing committee can check the writer's work.
3. Persons who have firsthand knowledge about a particular portion of the history can be asked to read first drafts.
4. Oral interviews can be checked for accuracy against other sources.
5. Newspaper stories and family histories, if used, need careful checking as to reliability.

Editing will involve insightful examination to see if goals were met. Were the guidelines followed? Did the writers adhere to the principles established at the beginning?

Was a consensus reached on how congregational conflicts would be handled in the history? The editor or advisory committee will notice how the writer dealt with problem areas. Is each portion truthfully presented? Have both sides of an issue been presented? Was the writer sensitive to differing viewpoints? Will the story encourage freedom of discussion? Will it build relationships and encourage forgiveness where needed?

Finally, editing includes checking spelling and grammar. Is the word usage correct? Is the sentence structure clearly formulated? Do the writer's ideas and analysis of data communicate as intended? Do the divisions of the book encourage readability? Do the titles and subtitles grab the attention of the reader? Does the language used limit the audience of the book or has care been taken to make the book readable and enjoyable? These and other points will be a part of the important work of editing the history.

Publishing

What type of product do you intend to produce? You will need to begin these plans early in the process. Will the congregation serve as publisher and hire only a printer? Or will a firm be contracted with for more responsibilities? There are certain advantages with either method. An editor of the publishing firm may do additional and concise editing; for example, determining divisions and titles in the book. A copy editor will check grammar and word usage. The book cover can be designed by a professional designer. The completed book will be listed in the firm's publishing catalog. The book will receive a Library of Congress number and an International Standard Book Number. The book may be copyrighted and will probably have a more polished and professional appearance.

Disadvantages for some congregations in using a publishing firm are that the higher cost may be impossible or not advisable for the budget. Also, the firm may require a higher number of copies printed than the congregation could readily sell.

Will the book be printed by a printing shop? Due to new types of printing, this method can cost far less per book. A clean copy of each page, with exact margins can be taken to the print shop. The printer will make as many copies as the congregation wishes. The printer will also provide choices of covers and if you have your cover designed, they will copy it for you and bind the book. The congregation may order the number of books desired and new orders can be placed though the cost may be much higher for a few more copies. The printing time is short, and the book is usually ready in far less time.

Many possible alternatives exist regarding the extent a congregation would employ a printer. Almost always in self-publishing, the congregation will be the publisher. This means they are responsible for all aspects of printing, marketing, and financing a book. The printer may do the type-setting (and thus layout) and copyediting of the manuscript. Or the printer may assist with various design aspects.

With self-publishing, the editorial assistance mentioned above from a publishing firm is not available. The book may not appear as polished in appearance.

With desktop publishing, the congregation provides camera-ready copy and only illustrations are needed. This will depend on whether the congregation, or a member, has desktop publishing equipment and also the necessary interest.

How many books will be published? This number will depend on many factors and the decision will be made by the historical committee or advisory committee with the congregation's help:

1. How large is the congregation?
2. How old is the congregation? Many former members may want copies.
3. Will there be broad community interest in the book?
4. Does the congregation intend to give the history to members or to those who attend the celebration event? This is sometimes possible in a self-publishing project.
5. Will members want to have copies for their children, grandchildren, or other extended family?
6. Will schools, colleges, libraries, and archives be interested?
7. Will church libraries of sister congregations want a copy? You may want to send several copies to your denominational library.

8. How many extra copies will be needed after initial sales? New members and ministers will want copies in the future. Will this history be updated in ten or fifteen years? Be realistic in your estimate. Some additional books will be needed; however, boxes and boxes of leftover books take up valuable space. Most congregations err on the side of printing too many because "500 copies cost only a little more than 300."

What will be the cost of the book? Will the book need to pay for itself? If so, then all costs related to committee expense, writing, editing, publishing, and advertising will be counted in the final cost.

Some congregations choose to pay some of the book costs from their budget. They can then set an arbitrary figure to be charged for the book. The most important factor should be to place the book in the hands of all who have an interest or who can benefit from the story.

Marketing

Market the book with this underlying message: "You will want a copy of this book. We want to share our story with you." Interest and involvement by the whole congregation can be stimulated from the book's conception to its completion and the final celebration. Marketing or placing the book will then be a natural step.

The youth group of the congregation may be successful at marketing the book. Older members like to see youth involved in the history and charging them with this responsibility will add to their sense of worth.

Other congregational organizations can also help. Perhaps a Sunday school class, women's or men's group will do the task. Be sure to have some group responsible for this part of the history project.

The marketing group may want to do prepublishing sales in order to help estimate the number of books for printing. This may also add interest as the book's arrival is awaited.

Advertising the book can be done throughout an anniversary celebration. Notices can be placed in bulletins, newsletters, and invitations for celebration events. Local newspapers could interview the writers for a news story. Regional and denominational papers will accept articles. Bookstores, both local and areawide, may be willing to sell the book for a reasonable commission.

The authors can participate in panel discussions and other types of programs. Displays about the book can be arranged in the church building or in a local store. A display at a meeting of several congregations can be worthwhile.

The arrival of the book is usually an exciting event. The congregation will respond to this festive occasion if kept informed during all the stages of its development. Flowers, banners, and displays can add to the mood of anticipation. A service of dedication can enhance the understanding that the history will make an important contribution to the members, individually and as a group. By searching the past and understanding how it has shaped the present, the congregation can grow in knowledge of who they are and what they have to offer.

Chapter 11

WHAT CAN WE LEARN FROM THE CELEBRATION?

One of the very real dangers in the post-celebration period is for the congregation to experience a "let down" feeling, especially when it has involved a lengthy time period. If the events of the celebration have climaxed in praise and thanksgiving, and all those involved provide a sense of joyous completion from successful efforts, why don't we sit back and relax over a job well done?

If we give in to this dangerous temptation, the celebration may become only a special event which we look back on with nostalgia. Unfortunately, we will not allow the celebration to enrich new mission and fresh inward and outward growth. How can we avoid the loss of forward movement?

Plan After-Celebration Activities

Before the climactic events of the celebration, the congregation needs to anticipate follow-up activities. This will promote a mind-set toward the future.

Evaluate the total celebration with the congregation. In an informal time of discussion, encourage all ages to participate in telling how the celebration has affected them.

What has been learned from it? Has the congregation benefited from working together?

Has it deepened relationships within the group? Has the story of the congregation from the past shown new truths about accomplishments?

Do members feel a fresh sense of identity or belonging to the congregation?

What were the favorite parts of all the events?

What stands out from the Sunday celebration as worthy of remembrance?

How did the celebration events affect visitors? former members? nonmembers?

How were decisions made? Does this need improvement?

If the celebration were to be repeated, what changes would the members recommend?

Write down everyone's ideas and remarks on a large sheet of paper. Publish this list in the church bulletin or in a newsletter. Include a copy of it in the anniversary records.

Celebrate what has been learned. Mention ideas gleaned from remarks, such as deepening relationships, old friendships renewed, or the joy of being together. Form these thoughts into a litany or guided meditation.

Collect impressions from members and nonmembers and put them in a scrapbook.

Use the names and addresses from the register and write thank-you letters to visitors.

Thank the congregation in some unique way—perhaps by having a party or picnic. Be sure to make this part of the "thank you," different from the events of the main celebration. Recognize the need to relax. If special meals have required long preparation, try hot dogs or purchasing fried chicken. Relax as you look forward and formulate new plans.

Continue Sharing with Nonmembers

What were the specific methods used to interact with nonmembers during the celebration? Which of these can be continued?

• Be attuned to enlarging the interests in your congregation which became evident during the celebration.

• Make follow-up visits to nonmembers who have shown interest in your congregation. Specific families may be encouraged to invite them to their homes or on outings. What are their vocational and hobby interests? What are their needs?

• Are there youth and children who would like to be a part of your group's activities?

• Are there single persons looking for a congregation to welcome them?

• Are there elderly persons who need rides to various places, including worship services? Do they feel lonely and need home visits? Try to use the celebration as a stepping stone to new mission.

Share the Congregation's Story with New Members

As persons come into the group, find ways of sharing the complete story of the congregation with them.

• At various times, show the videos and slide sets of celebration events.

• Acquaint persons with the history of the church as part of orientation sessions. Too often established members assume that new members know all about the organization and work of the congregation and leave them feeling on the fringe of the group. Make specific plans to include them.

• New ministers coming to the congregation after the celebration will find a wealth of material from many sources if events were carefully documented. Be sure the history is available to them in book or pamphlet form as well as photographs, scrapbooks, and videos. Have an informal program in which the congregation tells the minister about the celebration. Do not forget to include the children and youth. Highlight the special moments including humorous ones.

Will the Celebration Strengthen the Group's Identity?

Working together in a common framework for the same goals usually strengthens unity. A sense of oneness comes along with identifying closely with one another. Encourage this identification in the following ways:

1. Direct local news media, as well as regional and denominational, to cover the celebration.
2. Continue to display some of the decorations, such as a quilt, banners, or pictures of charter members.
3. Display articles from the main events, perhaps informal pictures taken of visitors and the congregation during the celebration. Copy pages from the register, showing the names of those who attended.
4. If necessary, make permanent the signs which had been placed to show the church's location to visitors.

As much as possible allow the celebration to be an ongoing source of praise, thanksgiving, and witness. Let it become a continuing means of binding the congregation together.

Has There Been Growth in Historical Collections?

Collections of all kinds which have come into existence through the celebration should be preserved. Adequate storage and display areas may be a needed new project. If possible, avoid the temptation to pack collections away in storage. Instead, arrange for them to augment the identity of the congregation by making them available to members and visitors.

Is There a Change in Records Management?

Has the congregation realized the importance of record keeping? Are there adequate means for safeguarding records? Will record keeping continue? To keep records for several occasions and then stop will not provide future members with a complete knowledge of the ongoing life and witness of the congregation. The celebration may create a new awareness of the importance of record management. When this happens it is truly an added benefit.

Make a Completed Time Line

Time lines have been a helpful tool throughout the celebration planning. There have probably been several: for planning the celebration; for preparing the congregation; for long-term and short-term events; for writing the history; and for the final day or days of main events.

Now, on looking back and seeing the celebration from its first conception to its final moments, it will be a valuable asset for the future, for a completed time line to be constructed. This will also be an excellent summary for the history records of the congregation.

Summary

This book has been written with several goals in mind:

1. to broaden the meaning of celebration for the readers by focusing on heritage as a gift from God
2. to place celebration in its proper theological position according to God's Word
3. to provide a broad resource from which congregations can choose the suggestions which seem to fit their pattern. We have given, therefore, very broad ideas, but at the same time tried to be specific.

We have noted several important points by stressing the need for:

1. careful planning
2. starting early
3. including a wide variety of persons
4. preserving the story through careful record keeping
5. gaining insights from the celebration that can be used for future mission and witness
6. Finally, we emphasized that the ultimate meaning of heritage celebration in the Christian Church lies in:
   a. thanksgiving and praise to God
   b. reconciliation and forgiveness based on Jesus Christ
   c. authentic vision for the future of God's kingdom which depends on knowing our past and allowing God to focus that knowledge so that we follow God's guidance in the present and future.

APPENDIX A

Anniversary Litany for Two Readers

1. We remember the families of yesterday, who dared to leave comforts and security to become a new community of faith, founded and established in Christ.
2. We thank God for their courage to face struggle, to conquer adversity; their willingness to live as strangers in a new land.
1. We recognize the enemies of faith which made them question their beliefs; the fears which drove them through humility to strength.
2. We thank God for the leadership he provided through seventy-five years of life; for the faith community which held out willing hands to others, and which nurtured life and love.
1. We thank God for grandparents who love us enough to affirm and warn us; who share their wisdom and faith with us.
2. We are grateful for parents who live their commitment daily in word and deed.
1. We are thankful for youth who ask questions and face the future with confidence; for children whose honesty and simple sincerity are examples to us.
2. We give you praise for brothers and sisters in the body of Christ who pray for us, forgive us, and share with us life's griefs and joys.

Written for the Seventy-fifth Anniversary of the Bethel Mennonite Church, Hydro, Oklahoma, July 3, 1981.

APPENDIX B

Historical Time Line

This time line covers the founding of this congregation, pastoral changes, and building projects. If starting dates for organizations within the congregation and their ongoing development were added, it would be an even more useful tool for the congregation.

1946	10/06/46	First regular service at Monterey.
	12/17/46	Officially organized with 37 charter members.
1948	04/04/48	Glenn Esh ordained as first pastor.
1950	11/15/50	Dedication of basement, reversed auditorium, and entrance.
1952	06/21/52	Maurice Landis and H. Hershey Balmer appointed to assist in the opening of the work at Neffsville.
1953		Addition of west wing at Monterey.
1960	05/02/60	Akron Mennonite Church formed with 46 charter members.
1965	06/20/65	Farewell dinner for Glenn Esh family (moved to Columbus, Ohio).
	07/04/65	Gordon Zook began pastoral ministry.
1969	11/01/69	Addition of mobile classroom.
1975	05/18/75	Congregation moved from Monterey to new building at Forest Hills.

1977	12/31/77	Gordon Zook resigned (moved to Elkhart, Indiana).
1979	06/17/79	Lester Graybill installed as pastor.
1982	09/26/82	Dedication of new education wing.
1984	08/15/84	Mark Wenger began as assistant pastor.
1986	10/04/86	40th anniversary of Monterey-Forest Hills Church.

Reprinted by permission from Rooted in Faith, Growing in Love: Forest Hills Mennonite Church 1946-1986, *by Abe Hallman.*

🌿

APPENDIX C

Questionnaire for Oral Interviews

Biographical Information

1. Name.
2. Date and place of birth.
3. Occupations throughout life.
4. Names of mother and father. When did they come here? Where did they come from? Were they involved in church work? What offices did they hold in church? in the denomination? Were they involved in politics? Did they vote? Did they take part in community activities? What kind?
5. How large were your parents' families? yours? Did your family speak another language at home? Does your immediate family speak another language? What papers were read by your parents? by you?
6. What church congregations did your parents belong to? Have you belonged to any other congregation?
7. What schools did your parents attend? What schools did you attend? Did you go to vacation Bible school?
8. At what age were you baptized? Did you take catechism or confirmation classes? How did you make the decision to become a follower of Christ? Was it a dramatic response to a call or did you feel you were nur-

tured over the years by church and family? Or was it both?

9. Looking back, what has been your greatest aid to spiritual growth? What has been the area of service in the church which has brought you the greatest joy?

Church Information

1. What has been the outstanding change you've seen in our church in the past fifty years?
2. What are the main issues facing our church today?
3. What do you see about our youth which is positive? negative?
4. What are the basic beliefs of the denomination that make you want to be part of it?
5. What is your prayer for our church in the future?

APPENDIX D

History Compilation Page

Year _____
Name of congregation _____
Reporter

Deaths:
  Name _____ Death date _____
    Birthday _____ Place buried _____
  Name _____ Death date _____
    Birthday _____ Place buried _____

Marriages:
  Name _____ and _____
    Place _____ Date _____
  Name _____ and _____
    Place _____ Date _____

Births:
  Name _____ Birth date _____
    Parents _____
  Name _____ Birth date _____
    Parents _____

Baptisms:
  Name _____ Baptism date _____
    Birth date _____

Name _____ Baptism date _____

     Birth date   _____

Transfers of membership:

Name _____ to _____

Name _____ to _____

Name _____ from _____

Name _____ from _____

Sunday school superintendent: _____

Assistant Sunday school superintendent: _____

Children's Sunday school superintendent: _____

Special Meetings:

Speaker _____ Date _____

Speaker _____ Date _____

Ordination:

Name _____ Date _____

Position _____

Average attendance:

Worship services _____

Sunday school _____

Bible school _____

Other changes:

_____

_____

_____

Compiled by Ada Nancy King, Atglen, Pennsylvania.

❧

APPENDIX E

Publishing Time Line

Early 1980	Editor appointed.
May 1980	Research and writing assignments given out.
October 30, 1980	Deadline for submitting writing assignments to editor.
December, 1980	Arthur L. Horting chosen as printer.
January 22, 1981	Began taking manuscripts to printer.
February 2, 1981	Printer started setting type.
February 17, 1981	Started proofreading first proofs.
March 8, 1981	Gave presentation of book in church.
March 25, 1981	Worked with printer in picture place ment.
April 9, 11, 1981	Spent evening and Saturday morning with printer, paginating the book (doing layout). Now we know how many pages there are—169.
April 14, 1981	Printer gave cost quotation for the book.
April 15, 1981	Committee decided on printing 700 copies at a cost of $6.40 per book.
May 6, 1981	Looked over page proofs of the book done by the printer's assistant.
May 12, 1981	Decided to use up some white space

	in the book by including very recent Belize report.
May 15, 1981	Were told there were seven blank pages at the end of the book.
May 16-18, 1981	Compiled and typed baptismal list ing for seven blank pages at end.
Mid-May 1981	Started printing.
May 26, 1981	Received final signature printing from printer.
Beginning of June	Printed pages sent to bindery.
June 10, 1981	Typed errata sheet—last and final feature of book.
June 15, 1981	Stumptown books arrived from bindery.
June 21, 1981	Books distributed at Stumptown, priced at $7.50 per book.

Compiled by Ivan and Mary Ellen Leaman, Lancaster County, Pennsylvania, detailing the publication of The Story of Stumptown Mennonite Church.

🦋

APPENDIX F

Indispensable Questions

Who . . .

1. Who were the people who created this congregation?
2. Who have been its leaders? its quiet pew sitters? its discontented members?
3. Who have been the people who joined the congregation?
4. Who left and why?
5. Who have been the people who wanted to change things in the congregation's life? Who wanted to keep things the same?
6. Who have been the spiritual people in the congregation? Who have served as its moral consciences? Who have been its status seekers and the power brokers?
7. Who have been the congregation's neighbors? Who has the congregation sought to keep out of its midst?
8. Who have shaped special interests of the congregation?
9. Who transmitted the congregation's identity and traditions to the next generation, and to newcomers?

What . . .

1. What did the founders set out to achieve when they formed this congregation? What have new members sought here?
2. What have been the congregation's official reasons for being, its official beliefs, its stances on moral, social, and theological issues?
3. What questions or problems have caused conflict in the congregation? What has been this congregation's style for dealing with controversy? What means has it used for resolving conflict?
4. What self-image has this congregation maintained?
5. What have been this congregation's distinctive customs, traditions, and values?
6. What has this congregation been especially proud of? What has it been embarrassed by?
7. What have been key turning points in the life of the congregation? What were the factors that shaped those events? What happened in their aftermath?
8. What has this congregation believed about God, society, itself, the individual?
9. What have been its greatest challenges? achievements? disasters? failures?
10. What has held this congregation together? What threatened to pull it apart?
11. What heritage has it treasured? What tradition(s) has it claimed? What values has it esteemed of which it is unaware?

When . . .

1. When did this congregation begin?

2. When has it experienced dramatic changes in membership?
3. When has it met for worship? for decision? for service? for social action?
4. When has it experienced controversy and turmoil?
5. When has it taken new direction? When has it reaffirmed old ways of doing things?
6. When has it been ahead of society as a prophet? When has it lagged behind as preserver of the status quo?
7. When have significant changes in leadership taken place?
8. When have new groups formed in the life of this congregation?
9. When has this congregation celebrated significant milestones in its life?
10. When will/did the life of this congregation come to an end?

Where . . .
1. Where did this congregation's members come from?
2. Where have new members come from?
3. Where has it built its buildings?
4. Where has it placed its priorities?
5. Where have lay leaders and clergy come from?
6. Where have members gone when they left this congregation?
7. Where have congregation members spent their time?
8. Where has it located its mission?

9. Where has this congregation turned for help or for resources for its ministry?
10. Where have new ideas come from in the life of the congregation?
11. Where have the congregation's most powerful competitors—both secular and religious—been found?

Why . . .

1. Why did this congregation come into being?
2. Why has it chosen the particular building design(s) it has? Why did it locate on this particular piece of earth?
3. Why have new leaders appeared on the scene? Why have old ones disappeared?
4. Why have this congregation's controversies or conflicts emerged when, where, and how they did?
5. Why have people continued/failed to join this congregation?
6. Why has this congregation made its significant changes—in worship, in organizational life, in membership requirements, in sense of mission, in sense of identity?
7. Why does this congregation handle its economic resources the way it does?
8. Why have people stayed in this congregation?
9. Why have young people dropped out at certain times in their lives and why have others seemed to join at particular moments in their life cycles?
10. Why have these people continued to gather, week in and week out?

How . . .

1. How has this congregation expressed its fundamental beliefs in specific practices?
2. How have membership patterns changed/stayed the same over the years?
3. How has power been distributed in this congregation?
4. How has this congregation made its decisions?
5. How has it spent its money?
6. How has it determined if it is succeeding or failing?
7. How has it responded to changes in society, denomination, neighborhood?
8. How has change been perceived in the congregation?
9. How has this congregation expressed its specialness?
10. How has this congregation told its story to new and younger members? How has it educated them or formed them spiritually?
11. How has this congregation expressed itself artistically, musically, theologically, socially?

Reprinted by permission from Places of Worship Exploring Their History *by James P. Wind (The Nearby History Series, American Association for State and Local History, Nashville, Tennessee), pages 40-43.*